Contents

The weird world of WEE

Imagine this: the Chinese soft-shelled turtle pees through its mouth.

The turtle is the only animal in the world that does this – but as you're about to find out, there are plenty of other creatures with interesting, unusual or just plain revolting wee habits.

THAT'S TURTLEY REVOLTING!

FIGHT! FIGHT! FIGHT!

If you're a lobster, wee is an essential part of getting a boyfriend or girlfriend. Male lobsters LOVE to fight – which makes it tricky to get close enough to fix a date ...

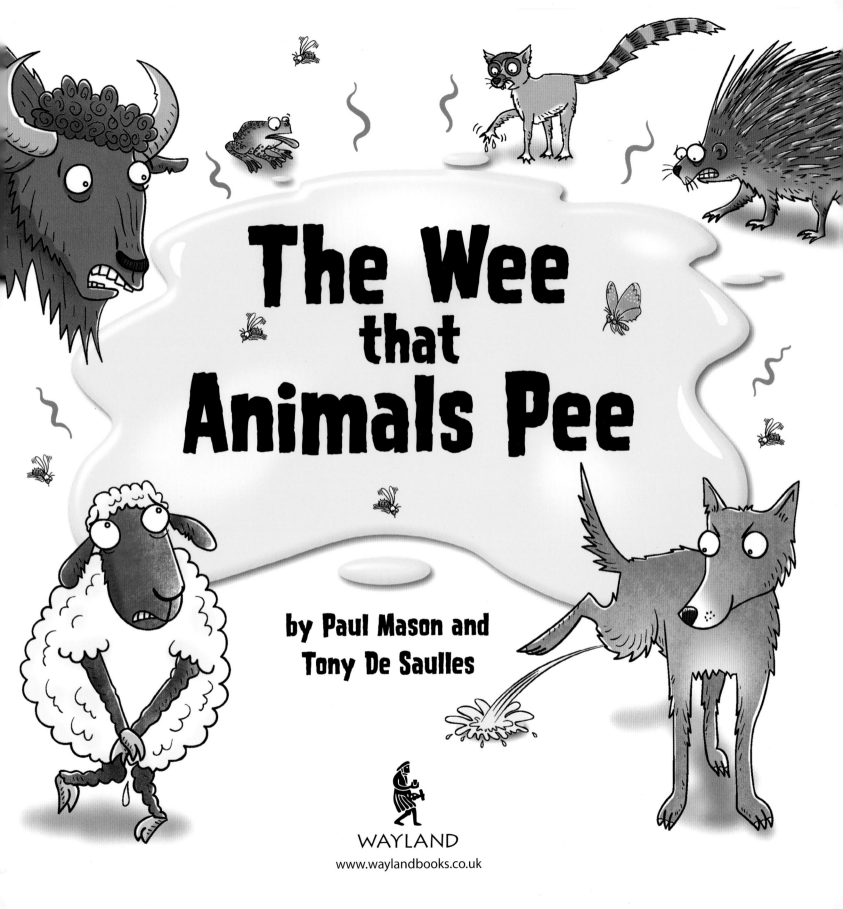

The Wee
that
Animals Pee

**by Paul Mason and
Tony De Saulles**

WAYLAND
www.waylandbooks.co.uk

First published in Great Britain in 2019 by Wayland
Text copyright © Hodder & Stoughton, 2019
Illustrations copyright © Tony De Saulles, 2019
All rights reserved.

Editor: Melanie Palmer
Designers: Peter Scoulding and Cathryn Gilbert
Picture researcher: Diana Morris

HB ISBN: 978 1 5263 0972 3
PB ISBN: 978 1 5263 0973 0

An imprint of
Hachette Children's Group
Part of Hodder & Stoughton
Carmelite House
50 Victoria Embankment
London EC4Y 0DZ

An Hachette UK Company
www.hachette.co.uk
www.hachettechildrens.co.uk

Printed in China

Picture credits:
Shutterstock: Andregric 17; Asharkyu 4t; Zvonimir Atletic 27b;
Bamgraphy 7c; Beersonic 20t; Rich Carey 28br; DashaR 26t;
Olga Grinblat 13c; Mikhail Holka 25b; Jiang Hongyan 18bl, 18br;
Szasz-Fabian Jozsef 15b; Kalcutta 7t; Kanyapak 11t; LoopAli: 20b;
MartinKSK_design 9b; Ed Phillips 7b; Saban Pumson 18t; Real
Moment 29t; Reptiles4all 22; Eni Sino 19c; Studiovin 24b; Sundays
Photography 12t; SuperPrin 6; Tomova 20c; USBFCO 16; E Walker
13cr; Zuzule 21b.
iStock: Marty8801 23.

The website addresses (URLs) included in this book were valid at
the time of going to press. However, it is possible that contents or
addresses may have changed since the publication of this book. No
responsibility for any such changes can be accepted by either the
author or the Publisher.

FSC
www.fsc.org
MIX
Paper from
responsible sources
FSC® C104740

So, the female lurks around the den of a male she likes the look of, peeing into it. The wee contains chemicals that show she's female. The chemical calms the male lobster down long enough to mate with the female.

COO-WEE!

WOULD YOU WEE-LIEVE IT?

As if finding the smell of wee relaxing isn't strange enough ... Lobsters pee out of their faces, from a place just below their ANTENNAE.

Time for some SCIENCE ...

What actually is wee? The story of how this dog came to be peeing on a lamppost explains:

RUFF!

kidney

salt

nitrogen

water

Trickle!

WEE!

① The dog went out for a walk and ran around.

② Waste products began to build up in the dog's blood. Poisonous NITROGEN and salt, plus water, were removed in the dog's kidneys.

③ From the kidneys, the waste and water (now called urine) travelled to the dog's BLADDER. This slowly filled up.

④ Now it has found a convenient lamppost, the dog is peeing out the waste.

Do all animals PEE?

Most animals need to get rid of nitrogen waste in some way. But what comes out of them is not always what you probably think of as wee.

Lightweight wee

Some animals need to be as light as possible. This means it is a really bad idea to carry around a bladder full of wee. Imagine a spider hanging on a thread, or a butterfly fluttering along.

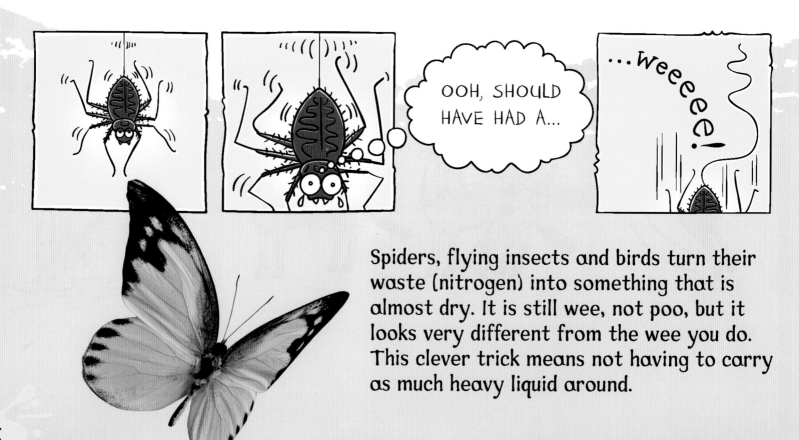

OOH, SHOULD HAVE HAD A...

...weeeee!

Spiders, flying insects and birds turn their waste (nitrogen) into something that is almost dry. It is still wee, not poo, but it looks very different from the wee you do. This clever trick means not having to carry as much heavy liquid around.

Non-peeing creatures

A few animals do not pee at all,
at least not for part of their lives.
They include:

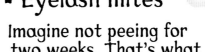

NO WEE
IN ME!

★ Eyelash mites

Imagine not peeing for
two weeks. That's what
the eyelash mite (which
lives in or near human
hair) does. The mites store
their waste inside their
own body.

WOULD YOU WEE-LIEVE IT?

Even though they have a liquid diet,
butterflies hardly pee. Instead, almost
all the liquid is extracted as part of
their DIGESTION.

HOLDING IT
ALL IN!

★ Bee larvae

Bee larvae store all
their wee until they
turn into bees.

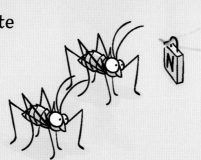

A little
for you...

★ Greenfly

Greenfly store their nitrogen waste
until they have young. Then they
put it into their children!
Greenfly have a lot of kids,
so each one only gets a bit
of nitrogen. At the end of
summer the greenflies die
and the rest of the nitrogen
they contain goes back
into the soil.

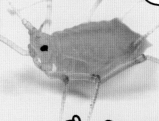

N is the chemical symbol for nitrogen.

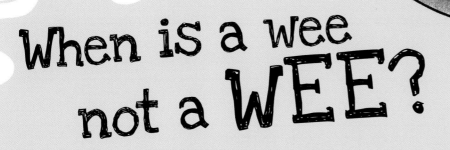

When is a wee not a WEE?

In humans and other MAMMALS, wee and poo are two separate things. You can wee without pooing and poo without weeing. Not all animals are like this.

In birds, amphibians, reptiles, sharks, rays and some other animals, wee and poo mix together. Then they leave the body through an opening called the cloaca.

Anyone who's ever had a bird dropping land on them would probably say it feels like being poo-ed on. In fact, what comes out of a bird's cloaca is usually more wee than poo.

WING SPAN OF PIGEON: HALF A METRE

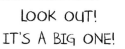

The white stuff is wee, actually.

LOOK OUT! IT'S A BIG ONE!

ARGH! BIRD POO!

The largest bird

The largest flying bird ever is *Pelagornis sandersi*. Its wingspan was over 7 metres and it must have produced huge droppings. You would NOT want to be underneath when Pelargornis decided to open its cloaca. Fortunately it died out 25 million years ago.

WING SPAN OF PELAGORNIS: 7.4 METRES

Bird-dropping face-packs

Most people would rather avoid bird droppings – but some celebrities can't get enough of them. As long as they're the droppings of a Japanese nightingale, that is.

UGH!

BIRD WEE! LUCKY ME!

Japanese nightingale

For hundreds of years people have claimed the droppings keep human skin looking healthy. Apparently the wee part of the droppings is essential, as it keeps your skin moist.

Today, nightingale droppings are made into a powder, mixed with other ingredients, and used as a FACE-PACK.

9

Is the SEA full of fish WEE?

Fish usually cannot leave the water, so they have no choice but to pee in the sea. Does that mean the sea is full of fish wee?

The short answer is no. Most fish release wee through their GILLS. Once it is in the sea, the wee starts to break down. The chemicals it contained spread out. In fact (despite what you might think at first) fish wee is a really good thing ...

Time for some SCIENCE ...

How can fish wee be good for the sea? This fish from a coral reef helps explain:

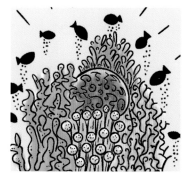

❶ This particular fish lives among an anemone's stinging tentacles. It is protected from them by a coating on its skin.

❷ As it swims, the fish releases wee from its gills. The wee spreads out into the water.

❸ The wee contains the chemicals phosphorus and ammonium. These sink down on to the coral reef.

❹ The corals use these chemicals for survival and growth. So, the fish's wee helps keep the reef strong.

Fishing, wee and coral reefs

Lots of fish have been caught by fishing boats on coral reefs. Because of this, there are fewer big fish peeing in the sea and the reefs are less healthy. The more fish, and fish wee, the healthier the surroundings. Fish wee helps seagrass meadows and kelp forests stay healthy.

> Oops! Sorry guys!

> UGH! It's Mr Smallbladder

Seahorses store their wee in a tiny bladder, before releasing it into the water.

The world's saltiest wee

Marine mammals such as whales and dolphins get some water from the bodies of fish they eat, but they also swallow a lot of salty water. Too much salt is harmful, so their bodies have to get rid of it. The salt is filtered out in their kidneys, moved to their bladder and released as some of the saltiest wee you could ever imagine.

Huge wees

The biggest animals in the oceans – whales – are also the biggest pee-ers. The largest whales are able to produce about 1,000 litres of wee every 24 hours.

> WATER'S WARM TODAY!

WOULD YOU WEE-LIEVE IT?

A large fin whale can be 27 metres long and weigh 20 tonnes. Every 24 hours it can produce 974 litres of wee.

You've got WEE-mail

Lots of animals use wee – or at least, the smell of wee – as a way of passing information to and fro. It's not email, it's wee-mail.

The smells section of a dog's brain is 40 times as big as yours.

For most humans, reading the messages in another person's wee would be impossible, because we don't smell that well. Many animals have a far better sense of smell than us, though.

How well can a dog smell?

Experts think dogs can smell between 1,000 and 10,000 times as well as humans. For a dog, smell is a more powerful sense than hearing or sight.

Dogs get all kinds of messages from the smell of another dog's wee:

REX WAS HERE

I'M NEW IN TOWN

I CAN WEE HIGHER THAN YOU (SO I'M BIGGER)

Marking your patch

Lots of animals mark the edges of their territory by peeing there. Experts think the smell says to others, 'This is our patch. Keep out.' Coyotes, tigers, beavers, mice, rats, foxes, cats and dogs all do this.

WOULD YOU WEE-LIEVE IT?

Dog wee contains chemicals that can rot metal. In 2003, peeing dogs were blamed for lampposts that started to fall over unexpectedly in Croatia.

Family news

White-footed lemurs live in family groups. At night, the lemurs feed alone. During the day they sleep in separate trees. So how do lemurs keep up with family news?

HOW'S IT GOING BRO?

The answer is wee. All the family go for a pee in similar places, though at different times. A good sniff brings them up to date with what everyone is up to.

PEE time!

Have you ever thought about how long you pee for, when you're really desperate (like when you wake up in the morning)? Because humans are mammals, the answer is probably about **20 seconds**.

Almost all mammals – apart from the smallest ones – pee for about this long if their bladder is full.

AFRICAN ELEPHANT	GREAT DANE DOG	PET CAT
Bladder holds 18 litres	Bladder holds 1.5 litres	Bladder holds 5 ml
Pee time: 21 seconds	Pee time: 24 seconds	Pee time: 21 seconds

How can an African elephant pee out 18 litres of wee as fast as a cat pees out a teaspoon full?

It is due to the width and length of the elephant's URETHRA, the tube from its bladder to the outside world. Wide urethras carry more wee (like a wide river carrying more water than a narrow stream). Longer urethras flow faster, as gravity has greater effect on the wee flowing down them.

Dribblers not Streamers

The 20-second rule does not apply to all mammals. The ones weighing less than 3 kg don't usually release a stream of wee. Instead they let out a quick burst or a series of drops. This is because their bladders are small so only hold a tiny amount of wee. They also need to pee quickly – if they stood still for 20 seconds, a predator might come and eat them!

PSSSSSSHHH!

1 ... 2 ... 3 ... QUICK, QUICK ... 4 ... 5 ... 6 ...

REVOLTING
facts (with rats)

Rats have SO many revolting wee habits. For a start, they pee on their own food.

If you can't vomit, pee instead

Why on earth do rats wee on their food? It is because they cannot VOMIT. If a rat swallows something poisonous, its body cannot get rid of it. Once it knows food is not poisonous, a rat pees on it as a signal that it's safe to eat. Young rats find the smell particularly hard to resist.

NIBBLE!   NIBBLE!

TUCK IN WHILE THE WEE'S STILL WARM!

SNIFF!

SNIFF!

WOULD YOU WEE-LIEVE IT?

Female rats use the smell of wee to find a boyfriend.

They can tell at a sniff whether a drop comes from the biggest, toughest male in town – or a weedy rat that's never won a fight and has a nasty disease.

Rat relations

As if they haven't done enough peeing already, rats also pee on each other in the following circumstances:

1. Female rats pee on possible boyfriends, so that they remember them later.
2. The toughest male rats pee on less-powerful ones.
3. The less-powerful male rats pee (carefully) on the toughest males.
4. Young rats pee on fully grown males – weirdly, this seems to be a way of STOPPING the adults attacking them.

SNIFF! SNIFF! OOH YEAH! I REMEMBER HIM!

Wee navigation

Rats leave little drops of wee on things and places they like. Some experts think they use the smell to navigate their way around – like a rat version of Hansel and Gretel, leaving a trail of white pebbles through the forest.

WEE weapons

In human society, peeing on someone would be quite likely to start a fight. In the animal world, it can work out the same way.

Fishy fighters

Some fighting fish let out a pee when they spot a possible enemy. If one fish smells that it is smaller and less powerful than the other, it usually swims off. If this doesn't happen, the fish pee more, to make sure their message has been sent. Only fish that are a similar size end up having a real fight.

NOOOO! A WATER PISTOL!

Rabbit rivals

EXCEPT IT'S NOT WATER!

Rabbits use a special, thick, strong-smelling wee for all kinds of things, such as to mark their home territory. Male rabbits pee on females they want as a girlfriend. When male rabbits fight, they may pee in each other's faces.

Doggy dominance

When a weaker dog meets a stronger one it signals by looking away, squatting down and letting out a little bit of wee. This is dog-speak for 'You're the boss, I don't want to fight.'

YOU SMELL!

Hair-raising hamsters

If there is one thing that annoys a male hamster, it is the smell of another male hamster's wee. As soon as they sniff it, they go into attack mode. First the hamsters start squeaking at each other. Then they start fighting. During the fight they often spray thick, smelly wee at each other.

WOULD YOU WEE-LIEVE IT?
RODENT wee glows in the dark. You'll need an ultraviolet torch to see it. If you shine the light around, any wee in the area glows blue-white or yellow-white.

Walking in WEE

Most humans would go quite a long way to avoid walking through wee – especially in their bare feet. Some animals, though, do it on purpose.

The popcorn-peeing bearcat

A bearcat is not actually a bear or a cat. It is a Southeast Asian mammal that looks a bit like a large weasel. The bearcat's proper name is binturong.

When it pees, it splashes all over its feet and bushy tail. The wee contains a special chemical called 2-AP. This is the same chemical that gives popcorn its mouthwatering smell. This means the binturong's wee-soaked footprints smell just like popcorn!

WHO ARE YOU CALLING A WEE-SEL?

YUMMY, SMELLS LIKE THE CINEMA!

Urine-loving ungulates

Ungulates are animals that have hoofs, for example cows, sheep, moose and bison. Many ungulates love nothing more than either:

1. to pee on their own legs

2. to wallow in mud soaked in their own wee. When the mud dries, the smell is really caked on!

Experts think the animals do this as a way of demonstrating strength. If they smell strongly of wee (the animals, not the experts), it means they are strong themselves. Other animals will take one sniff and give way.

STALLIONS spread their wee around for the same reason – but they do it on their herd's dung piles, rather than themselves.

21

Where is the WEE?

NNNNG!

Some animals live in very dry places. They don't really like to release liquid that might be useful later, so they keep it inside for as long as possible.

Wee like treacle

A jerboa is a weird-looking desert creature. It's a little rodent that is like a cross between a bat (big ears), a mouse (head and body) and a miniature kangaroo (hoppy legs).

Ugh, so humiliating!

BAT EARS

MOUSE BODY

HOPPY LEGS

TREACLE WEE

Jerboas survive without drinking: they get moisture from their food and keep as much inside as possible. Before they have a pee, their kidneys reabsorb water from their urine. What comes out is more like treacle than wee.

Australian desert frogs

A desert is not a place you'd expect to find frogs. In Australia's deserts, though, there are surprising numbers of frogs in the bone-dry landscape. They survive by digging below the surface and waiting for rain. The frogs store water inside their body, including lots of wee in their bladder.

WOULD YOU WEE-LIEVE IT?
Thirsty travellers have been known to dig up desert frogs, then squeeze out the water for a drink.

Pleeeeease rain or I'm gonna croak!

Desert tortoise

The Mojave Desert tortoise is another wee-saving animal. When it rains, the tortoise drinks as much as it can from puddles. It stores the water in the form of wee in its bladder. A tortoise can hold almost half its body weight in this way. This allows it to survive long periods without drinking.

When threatened, the tortoise empties its bladder. This is a good reason not to pick up a desert tortoise, if you ever meet one!

Ah, how sweet!

23

Keeping WEE-ly clean

For hundreds of years, humans have used wee for a variety of jobs. Sometimes they use animal wee, sometimes their own.

Clothes and cleaning

In some places, wee is still used today as part of the process for making leather. It contains chemicals that soften animal skins, making them easier to sew and more comfortable to wear.

Wee also contains chemicals that remove stains, so in the past it was used as a kind of washing liquid. One of the worst jobs in ancient Rome must have been stomping dirty clothes in vats of watered-down wee to clean them.

WOULD YOU WEE-LIEVE IT?

The Romans didn't only use wee for cleaning clothes – they also used it as a tooth-whitener.

Hurry up I want to go to bed!

24

Thank you, babies! Now that's what I call POTTY POWER!

Exploding wee

Through a complicated process of mixing and boiling, you can use a lot of wee to make a tiny bit of PHOSPHOROUS. Phosphorus burns fiercely when it comes into contact with air, so it is a dangerous substance.

Wee also contains chemicals that can be used to make saltpetre – a crucial ingredient in GUNPOWDER.

Wee medicine

Since ancient Greek times, people have been claiming that wee has health benefits. It has been used as medicine in Europe, India and China. Sometimes the 'cure' was to drink it. Sometimes it was used to treat wounds. The treatments were all more likely to make you ill than make you well. Wee is clean when it leaves the bladder, but as soon as it leaves the body it starts to develop BACTERIA. Drinking or rubbing on bacteria – which cause diseases – is not a good idea.

25

WEE power

Although humans have been finding ways to use animal wee for thousands of years, they are still coming up with new ones today.

Heat from horse wee

Barn House in Japan is an experimental home heated partly by horse wee. First, the horses' poo is collected and turned into FERTILISER. Then their wee, plus some sawdust, is added. When dried in the sunshine the mixture forms CHARCOAL, which is burned to heat the house.

Of course, the NEIGHHHBOURS complained about the smell!

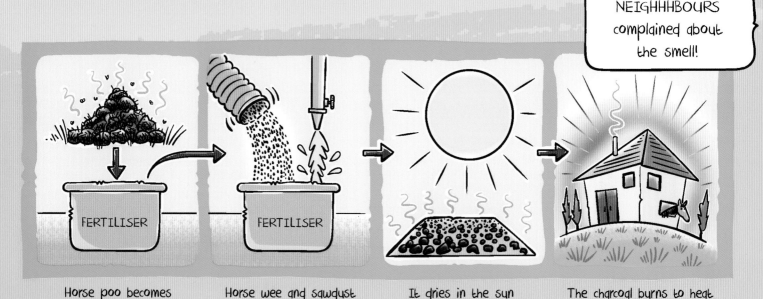

Horse poo becomes fertiliser

Horse wee and sawdust are added to the mixture

It dries in the sun and becomes charcoal

The charcoal burns to heat the house

Wee-powered phones

In Bristol, UK, scientists have come up with a way to make electricity from wee. The system is based around tiny living creatures called microbes. The microbes like nothing more than a meal of wee. As they eat, the produce a tiny amount of electricity. In 2013, the scientists managed to collect the electricity and use it to charge a mobile phone for the first time. Maybe it should be called electrici-wee?

Burning wee

In Nigeria, four schoolgirls have invented a device that turns wee into useable fuel. It works by removing a chemical called hydrogen from wee, then purifying it. The hydrogen can then be burned as fuel. A litre of wee can provide up to six hours of power.

Cow wee insecticide

In India, cow wee is being used as an INSECTICIDE, keeping insects off farmers' crops. The chemicals in the wee are broken down by bacteria, then mixed with special leaves that insects do not like. The mixture is then added to crops. As an extra bonus, the nitrogen contained in cow wee helps to fertilise the soil.

Mythical WEE

There are lots of strange stories about wee. Here are a few, plus explanations of whether or not you should believe them.

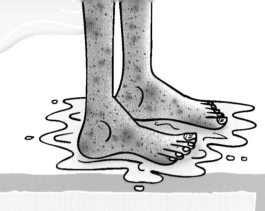

YOU SHOULD PEE ON A JELLYFISH STING

Around the world, people will tell you to pee on a jellyfish sting to stop it hurting. Don't listen! It is definitely not the right thing to do. Peeing on the sting may cause the little jellyfish stingers on your skin to release even more VENOM. The best thing to do is wash the sting with seawater.

THE TREES IN LONDON/NEW YORK/PARIS SURVIVE ON DOG WEE

This story says that in many cities, the trees would die if they weren't always being watered by dog wee. This is not true. Trees mostly draw water up from their roots, not through their bark. A dog peeing on the bark does not help a tree. In fact, some experts think the chemicals in dog wee may actually damage trees, especially young ones.

Seawater not wee water!

EVERYTHING WILL BE FINE, IT'LL BE OK, IT'LL BE FINE, IT'LL BE OK ...

FROGS ALWAYS PEE ON YOU WHEN YOU PICK THEM UP

This one is true, they nearly always do. The frogs are peeing to make you put them down again, so they can escape. Some frogs have particularly nasty-smelling wee that is specially discouraging. It also tastes terrible, to encourage predators to spit the frog out quickly.

ONLY MALE CATS SPRAY THINGS WITH WEE

Spraying is when a cat pees on something: a wall, sofa, bed, carpet or pile of laundry for no obvious reason except to make it smell. Many people think only male cats spray, but this is wrong. When cats are worried, they spray wee everywhere. They do it to reassure themselves that they are in a safe place. Because male and female cats can both get worried, they both spray.

I mean, COME ON! Can you blame me?

29

WEE-ly good facts

It would take 12 mice about a day to fill a teaspoon with wee.

Despite the stories, camels do not store water in their humps. Their wee contains much less water than other animals', which makes it as salty as seawater. When they do pee, camels do it all over their legs to help keep them cool.

Siberian chipmunks like to cover themselves in snake wee, as a kind of stinky camouflage.

Reindeer drink urine because it contains salt, and salt is rare in the northern lands where they live. In fact, reindeer herders sometimes pee as a way of gathering their herds. The reindeer smell the wee and come running.

Baby bears born in a den in winter do not go outside until spring. When they feed, their mother licks up their wee to keep the den clean.

There are lots of words for peeing. The scientific one is micturition. It is also called urination, voiding, emiction and pissing. 'Piss' is thought to come from an old French word, *pissier*, which means 'urinate'.

Glossary

antennae long, thin stalks on the heads of some animals, which they use for sensing the world around them

bacteria tiny living things made of just one cell. Bacteria are everywhere and some of them transmit diseases

bladder a pouch inside the body where wee collects, before being pee-ed out when the bladder becomes full

charcoal black fuel made from wood, which produces heat when burned

digestion removal of things the body needs from food once it has been eaten

face-pack something smeared temporarily on a person's face in the hope it will improve the skin

fertiliser something that helps plants to grow bigger or more quickly

gills parts of a fish or an amphibian's body that removes oxygen from water

gunpowder grainy black or grey substance that, when lit, releases energy in an explosion

insecticide substance used to kill or scare off insects

mammal animal with hair or fur and whose young are fed with their mother's milk

nitrogen chemical contained in soil, air and water

phosphorus chemical that glows in the dark and catches light when exposed to air

rodent largest group of mammals, which have teeth designed for gnawing and include rats, mice, porcupine, hamsters and squirrels

stallion male horse that is capable of mating with a female to produce young

urethra the tube down which wee flows from the bladder to outside an animal's body

venom poison injected into a victim, for example by some snakes, spiders and insects

vomit be sick or throw up

Index